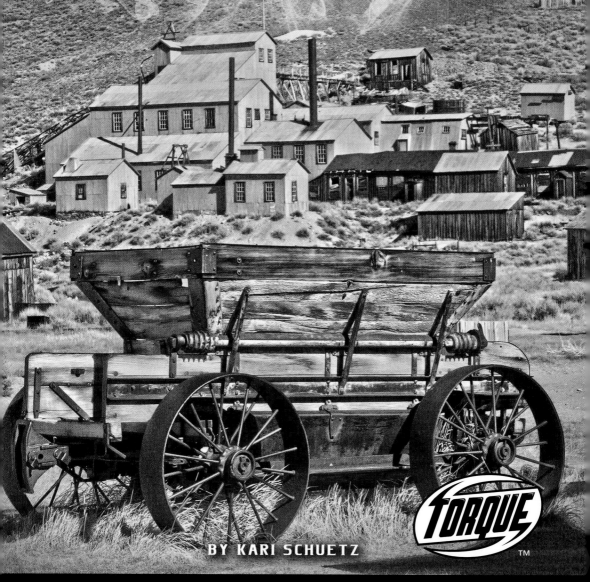

ABANDONED PLACES

BODIE

THE GOLD-MINING GHOST TOWN

BY KARI SCHUETZ

TORQUE™

BELLWETHER MEDIA • MINNEAPOLIS, MN

Are you ready to take it to the extreme?
Torque books thrust you into the action-packed world
of sports, vehicles, mystery, and adventure. These
books may include dirt, smoke, fire, and chilling tales.
WARNING: read at your own risk.

This edition first published in 2018 by Bellwether Media, Inc.

No part of this publication may be reproduced in whole or in part without written
permission of the publisher. For information regarding permission, write to Bellwether
Media, Inc., Attention: Permissions Department, 5357 Penn Avenue South,
Minneapolis, MN 55419.

Library of Congress Cataloging-in-Publication Data

Names: Schuetz, Kari, author.
Title: Bodie : The Gold-mining Ghost Town / by Kari Schuetz.
Description: Minneapolis, MN : Bellwether Media, Inc., [2018] | Series:
  Torque: Abandoned Places | Includes bibliographical references and index.
  | Audience: Ages 7-12. | Audience: Grades 3-7.
Identifiers: LCCN 2016057237 (print) | LCCN 2016057441 (ebook) | ISBN
  9781626176942 (hardcover : alk. paper) | ISBN 9781681034249 (ebook)
Subjects: LCSH: Bodie (Calif.)–Gold discoveries–Juvenile literature. |
  Bodie (Calif.)–History–Juvenile literature. | Frontier and pioneer
  life–California–Bodie–Juvenile literature. | Ghost
  towns–California–Juvenile literature.
Classification: LCC F869.B65 S38 2018 (print) | LCC F869.B65 (ebook) | DDC
  979.4/48–dc23
LC record available at https://lccn.loc.gov/2016057237

Editor: Betsy Rathburn   Designer: Brittany McIntosh

Printed in the United States of America, North Mankato, MN.

TABLE OF CONTENTS

THE CURSE OF BODIE

Here you stand in Bodie, one of the wildest towns of the Old West. Its streets are deserted now. But the run-down remains connect you to the past.

Your eyes search the ground for leftover gold. But then you remember the Curse of Bodie. Could you be doomed to bad luck if you take something from the town?

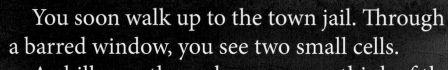

You soon walk up to the town jail. Through a barred window, you see two small cells.

A chill runs through you as you think of the lawless prisoners once locked inside. Do the ghosts of robbers and gunslingers haunt this town? Bodie's wild past still makes the town feel alive!

Bodie jail

BOOMTOWN OF THE WILD WEST

Bodie is a Wild West **ghost town** in California. It is located just east of the Sierra Nevada mountain range. **Miners** built the town high in the hills during the state's **gold rush**.

Since 1962, the abandoned town has been an official historic site. The California park system protects the buildings left standing.

Bodie, California

N
W E
S

Treeless Town

Bodie sits above the tree line at a height of 8,375 feet (2,553 meters). Trees do not grow there.

Bodie in the late 1800s

Back when it was a boomtown, Bodie had a wild reputation. The gold attracted a rough crowd.

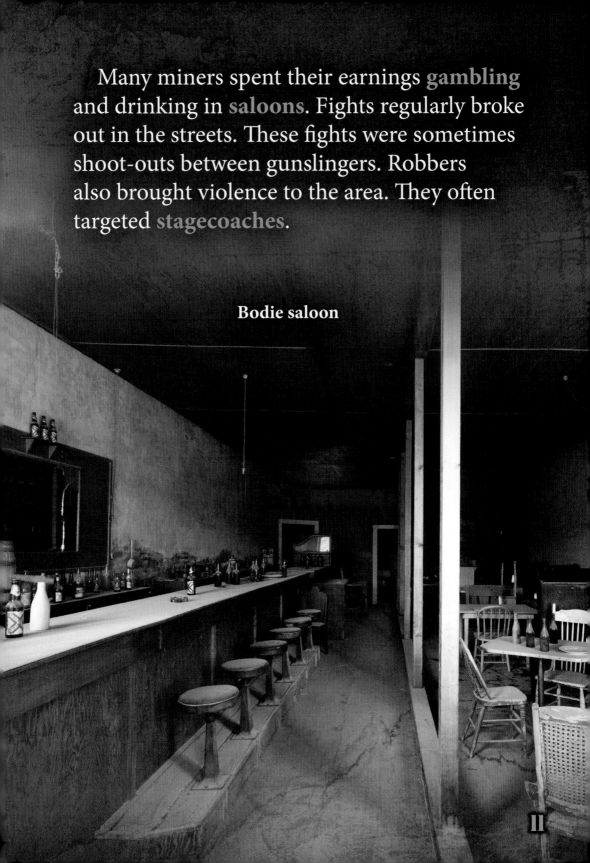

Many miners spent their earnings gambling and drinking in saloons. Fights regularly broke out in the streets. These fights were sometimes shoot-outs between gunslingers. Robbers also brought violence to the area. They often targeted stagecoaches.

Bodie saloon

A CALIFORNIA GOLD RUSH

W.S. Bodey first put Bodie on the map in 1859. He was one of four prospectors who found gold in the area.

Spell It Like This

Two different stories explain how Bodey became Bodie. One says that a sign painter introduced the –ie spelling. The other says that townspeople changed the spelling to help newcomers pronounce the name.

But just months after the find, Bodey died in a blizzard. He never saw the mining camp that formed in 1861. Still, the town of Bodie was named after him.

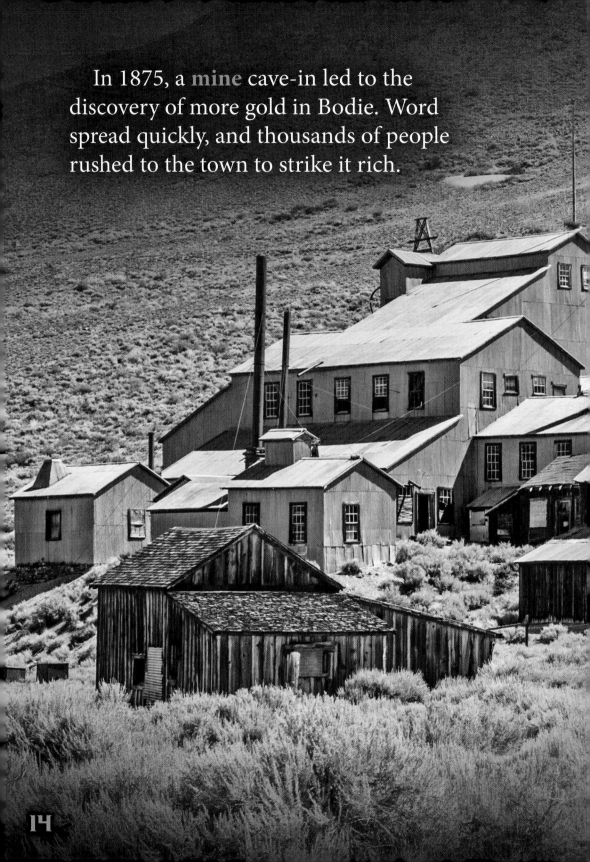

In 1875, a **mine** cave-in led to the discovery of more gold in Bodie. Word spread quickly, and thousands of people rushed to the town to strike it rich.

Wood Wanted

The Bodie and Benton Railway connected the town to a lumber mill. The mill provided the wood Bodie needed for building, heat, and power.

Bodie's population grew from 20 miners to nearly 10,000 people by 1880. At its peak, the town had 30 gold mines.

The big rush lasted into the early 1880s. Then mines started to shut down. By 1890, only a couple were still open.

Then businessman J.S. Cain introduced a new type of mining to Bodie. The process used a chemical called cyanide. This new approach kept the town alive for a little longer.

BODIE TIMELINE

1859:
Prospectors first discover gold in the Bodie area

1875:
A mine cave-in leads to a large gold discovery in Bodie

Millions in Gold
Bodie mines produced over $32 million in gold!

1877:
The big rush of fortune seekers coming to Bodie begins

1892:
Fire destroys much of Bodie

1880:
The town of Bodie is in its peak period with almost 10,000 people and 30 mines

BECOMING A GHOST TOWN

When the mines were used up, Bodie's downfall began. The town had little to offer once the gold was gone. Miners left when they could not find work.

Bodie in 1918

Buildings Still Standing

During boom time, Bodie had around 2,000 buildings. Today, just over 100 of these remain in the state park.

Soon, **Prohibition** forced saloons to close. Then by 1932, fire had destroyed 95 percent of Bodie.

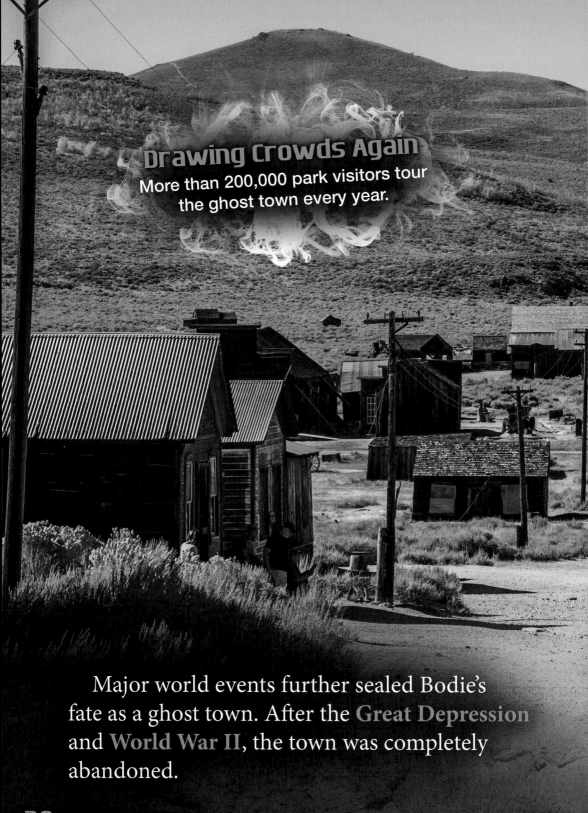

Drawing Crowds Again

More than 200,000 park visitors tour the ghost town every year.

Major world events further sealed Bodie's fate as a ghost town. After the Great Depression and World War II, the town was completely abandoned.

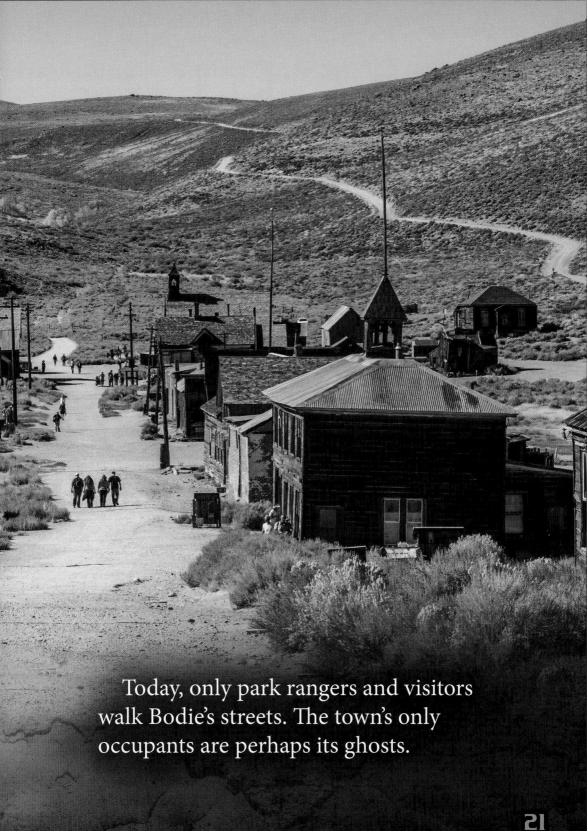

Today, only park rangers and visitors walk Bodie's streets. The town's only occupants are perhaps its ghosts.

GLOSSARY

boomtown—a town that has a sudden population increase due to business growth

gambling—betting money on games with unpredictable outcomes

ghost town—a town that once flourished but is now deserted

gold rush—a sudden movement of people looking for riches to an area where gold has been discovered

Great Depression—the period in the 1930s when businesses struggled and unemployment was high

mine—an underground tunnel or pit from which gold or another mineral is taken

miners—workers who dig for gold or other natural resources

Prohibition—the ban on making or selling alcohol in the United States during the 1920s and early 1930s

prospectors—people who search for natural deposits of gold

reputation—the way a place is viewed based on the behavior of its people

saloons—places where adults hang out to drink alcohol

stagecoaches—wheeled vehicles pulled by horses

World War II—a war fought from 1939 to 1945

TO LEARN MORE

AT THE LIBRARY

Blake, Kevin. *Bodie: The Town That Belongs to Ghosts.* New York, N.Y.: Bearport Publishing, 2015.

Landau, Elaine. *The Gold Rush in California: Would You Catch Gold Fever?* Berkeley Heights, N.J.: Enslow Publishers, Inc., 2015.

Parvis, Sarah. *Ghost Towns.* New York, N.Y.: Bearport Publishing, 2008.

ON THE WEB

Learning more about Bodie is as easy as 1, 2, 3.

1. Go to www.factsurfer.com.

2. Enter "Bodie" into the search box.

3. Click the "Surf" button and you will see a list of related web sites.

With factsurfer.com, finding more information is just a click away.

INDEX